ONE.

"Degenerated," by the band Reagan Youth, is a perfect punk song. It clocks in at just two minutes and twenty-two seconds on the album version. It has a killer riff, relentless drums, and a catchy, snotty vocal hook. The lyrics—sung by Dave Insurgent—tell the story of a teenager named Johnny, who can't read or write, and is only concerned with the momentary thrills of sex, drugs, and television.

Dave Insurgent (David Rubinstein) and Paul Cripple (Paul Bakija) hashed out the first, rudimentary version of the song in 1979, the summer before they started high school. In that first version, the song featured more juvenile lyrics, and no doubt less than professional instrumentation, but over a solid half-decade of rehearsing the song, and performing it live around New York City, it solidified into its complete form. The song was initially recorded in 1984 for the Rat Cage Records release, *Youth Anthems for the New Order*, then re-mastered by New Red Archives in 1988 for the revamped version of *Youth Anthems*, known as *Volume 1.*

In this final form, "Degenerated" became a classic punk anthem, a brutal and ironic attack on brain dead American youth. Like all anthems, though, especially ironic ones, it can easily be reduced to meaninglessness. Many people recognize the song today as it was covered in the Hollywood comedy *Airheads*, as a straightforward metal song. Even when performed by Reagan Youth, it is easy to take out of context as on embracement of mindless teen aggression.

My favorite version is a very contextualized live recording. It was recorded at CBGB one afternoon in1983, and can be found on the *Live & Rare* compilation (New Red Archives). Despite being hailed as the birthplace of punk, CBGB as a business was never completely comfortable with the punks themselves. With the second wave of punk in the early 80s, the punks became younger, more vicious, more hardcore. CBGB's solution was to hold weekend matinees, where underage kids (sixteen and over) could come, pay admission, and do their thing, while still being cleared away before a drink-buying crowd showed up at night.

The recording captures the feel of the matinee show. Though the mix is taken right from the soundboard, you can still hear all the kids singing along with the chorus, in the background through Dave's microphone. They are young and they are excited. Paul Cripple's guitar is fuzzier, not as blazing as on the studio version, but the riff is heavy and it sounds great. When the drums (Al Pike) and bass (Steve Weissman) kick in, you can feel the whole room dancing. It's a hell of a lot of energy packed into two minutes and twenty-seven seconds.

What is most important to me about this particular recording, though, is Dave's stage banter. Banter isn't quite the right word. It's proclamation, testimony, public confession. He speaks before the song, during the bridge, and at the end of the song, offering his personal counter-narrative. This autobiographical story—spoken honestly, in his Queens accent—is not as forceful as the sung verses of Johnny's pathetic life. But Dave is telling his own story with earnestness, struggling to have it be the truer story.

"Alright," he starts. "This is going out to whoever wants to hear it." Paul Cripple starts playing the riff. "Sitting out in Queens, I was in a schoolyard doing a lot of drugs. Like mescaline, and stuff. And ludes." Dave takes a breath, transitioning from speaking to a shout: "I was a teenage zombie!" As of now, Dave's story still mirrors Johnny's. The drums and bass come in behind the riff, giving it solidity and speeding it up. Dave begins to sing the first lyrics of the song: "What's Johnny doing on Tuesday night?"

At the minute and a half mark, Paul Cripple starts galloping, going as far into a melodic metal solo as one can in the twenty-second bridge of a punk song, when you have no rhythm guitar to back you up. It's an earned solo. Over it, Dave's owns story takes a turn:

"So I was sitting in this fucking schoolyard, getting dope. And then punk came along and made me a human." He says "human" slow, in two parts ("hu-MAN") like it is a word he is just learning. "There is an answer!"

Paul snaps back into the main riff, and Dave launches into the last verse of the song, where Johnny becomes a spent, TV-watching dad, who has spawned an even more degenerated son. The end of the verse builds and builds, then abruptly stops. There is no final chorus.

"And then I found out about punk." Dave says. Al Pike plays three descending notes on his bass. "The saga unrolls..."

The saga would unroll tragically, over the next ten years. Hardcore punk became more insular and violent. So many punks, including Dave, became addicted to heroin. Dave, his girlfriend, and mother all died tragically within ten days of each other. The Lower East Side of New York City was forcibly gentrified. The entire city became a militarized police state, a situation that persists to this day. And yet, listening to the live recording, it is difficult to be entirely disheartened. You believe Dave Insurgent. You trust him. Punk Rock is the answer.

TWO.

One of the problems with the punk subculture is our willful lack of context. As Guy Picciotto sings in the Fugazi song, "Bulldog Front": "Ahistorical—you think this shit just dropped right out of the sky."

When we do consider our past, it is often to mythologize and idealize long gone scenes, and to create hagiographies of kids who died young. Rarely do we consider the realities and contexts that formed these scenes, or, for that matter, our own scenes.

As a punk kid growing up in suburban West Philadelphia in the 1990s, I sang along to songs from the Reagan Era—by bands like Reagan Youth and the Dead Kennedys—without really understanding the context that had given rise to them. Later, when I moved to New York City as an older teenager, I began to hear, and repeat, the legends of the old Lower East Side scene. I looked to these tales as benchmarks of authenticity, never stopping to consider them in a deeper or more nuanced fashion.

Punk has taken many forms in the past three-and-a-half decades, and each of these forms exists in the historical context of punk, the historical context of other subcultures, and the historical context of the dominant culture. If punk is going to continue to mean anything, it will only be because we are willing to question its past and future, and continue to imbue it with new meaning.

THREE.

Punk is obviously a very regional subculture, and every scene has its own identity, history, and sense(s) of self. These scenes exist within cities. We can leave our neighborhoods and family names behind as we come together in a new community, but we inevitably bring the issues we grew up with us.

New York City is an immigrant city. There are currently close to three million immigrants in New York City, not to mention the millions more who are the American-born children of immigrant families. With the partial exception of the period from the mid-1920s to the mid-1960s, when racist national immigration policies severely limited immigration to the United States, huge numbers of people have been continually immigrating to New York City. This does not mean that the city is a melting pot; ethnic, religious, racial, and class divisions continue to segment the city, often on a block-by-block level. What it does mean is that New York is a city of people dealing with trauma: the traumas we fled, the trauma of immigration itself, and the traumas we inherit from our parents. Dave Insurgent was a prime example of this.

Dave Insurgent's father, Adolph Ronald Rubinstein, was born in Krakow, Lesser Poland, in 1913. As an educated, affluent, assimilated Jew, coming of age in an urban center of the Second Polish Republic, the doors to all that modern Europe had to offer stood open for Rubinstein.

These doors slammed shut on September 1, 1939 with the Nazi invasion of Poland. Two weeks later, Poland was attacked from the other side by Germany's new ally, the USSR. The twenty-six year old Rubinstein, a member of the Polish Army, was sent to a Soviet Gulag, as were over 200,000 other Polish prisoners of war. Thousands of other Polish prisoners—including the more than twenty thousand victims of the Katyn massacre—were murdered outright by Stalin's secret police, The NKVD.

In 1941, Hitler invaded Russia, invalidating the Molotov pact. The Soviet Union reestablished diplomatic ties with Poland and freed the Polish prisoners of war, allowing them to form an army in exile under the leadership of General Wadyslaw Anders (who himself was only recently released from two years in the Lubyanka prison, where he was tortured by the NKVD).

Though officially the Second Polish Corps, the army soon came to be known as Anders' Army. In his memoirs, Anders recalls the condition of the troops as they first assembled:

> I shall not forget the sight as long as I live, nor the mingled pity and pride with which I reviewed them. Most of them had no boots or shirts, and all were in rags, often the tattered relics of old Polish uniforms. There was not a man who was not an emaciated skeleton and most of them were covered with ulcers, resulting from semi-starvation, but to the great astonishment of the Russians, including General Zhukov, who accompanied me, they were all well shaved and showed a fine soldierly bearing.

The fact that Sid Vicious' father was a Beefeater, or Yeoman Warder, at Buckingham Palace is an oft-repeated bit of punk lore. Where Vicious rebelled against a father who stood at attention in a tourist camera-ready red uniform, Insurgent rebelled against a father who led drills in the Russian winter, wearing the shreds of a uniform of a country that no longer existed.

After months of training with wooden rifles on subsistence rations, Anders' Army was outfitted with uniforms and real rifles, and began a long trek (along with thousands of orphaned Polish children) to Tehran, Iran, which was jointly occupied by Great Britain and the USSR. Following the revelation of the Katyn massacre in 1943, Stalin cut off all ties with the Polish government-in-exile.

At this point, Anders' Army passed into the auspices of the British Military. In this capacity, they saw combat on the Italian front, where Ander's observed that: "Corpses of Polish and German soldiers, sometimes entangled in a deadly embrace, lay everywhere, and the air was full of rotting bodies."

Later, Anders' Army would march on to the British Mandate of Palestine. Many Jewish soldiers from the army remained in Palestine (legally or illegally), and became involved in the Haganah, the illegal Jewish paramilitary organization that would later form the core of the Israel Defense Forces. Rubinstein, however, chose to remain under British command, eventually taking a commission with the British Army as an intelligence officer. By the end of the war, there was no home to return to; the Jewish population of Poland had been almost entirely destroyed, and Poland itself was under communist control. Ronald eventually immigrated to New York, to reunite with surviving cousins. He became a citizen of the United States in 1954.

Giza (Gitla) Patt was born in Lodz, Poland in 1927. At the time, Lodz was the second largest Jewish community in Poland, as well as in Europe. Giza was only twelve years old when the Nazis invaded Poland in 1939. In 1940, the city's 160,000 Jews were forced into a newly created ghetto. The Patt family was relocated from their comfortable home in the heart of Lodz, to Sulzfelder Strasse in the ghetto.

Lodz was an important industrial center in pre-war Poland, and the Nazis took advantage of this by constructing dozens of factories in the ghetto and staffing them with Jewish slave laborers, who were often literally worked or starved to death. Deportations from Lodz Ghetto to the concentration camps began in 1942, but the Germans kept the ghetto intact until 1944 (after the other ghettos in Poland had been liquidated), because of the high rate of production.

The final deportations from the Ghetto took place in the summer of 1944, and Giza herself was deported to a concentration camp (either Dachau or Auschwitz). Giza survived the camps but her parents were murdered by the Nazis.

After the war, eighteen-year-old Giza ended up as a refugee in Israel. After a brief, unhappy marriage, she made her way to New York, where she met Ronald Rubinstein. The Rubinstein's only child, David, was born in 1964. Ronald (he did not use the name Adolph) worked as a colorist for the *New York Times* Sunday Magazine, and the family settled in Rego Park, a middle-class neighborhood in Queens. Rego Park was developed in the 1920s by the Real Good Construction Company (a contraction of the words "Real Good" gives the neighborhood its name), and its comfortable, single-family houses became home to many upwardly mobile immigrant families. Many of the immigrants who settled there in the post-war period were Holocaust survivors; it is not a coincidence that much of Art Spiegleman's graphic novel, *Maus*, takes place in the neighborhood. By 1964, though, the horrors of the war were almost two decades in the past. The Rubinsteins had built a new life for themselves, and hoped to give their American-born son everything that had been taken from them in Poland.

Ronald and Giza were extremely protective parents. Rego Park and the adjacent Forest Hills (where Dave attended junior high), were safe neighborhoods by the standards of 1970s New York City, but to Holocaust survivors like the Rubinsteins, the world would always be an extremely dangerous place. While other kids in the neighborhood would spend their evenings and weekends running around and playing football, Dave was often stuck at home.

Spending time alone in his parents' house, Dave began to develop the interests that he would pursue for the rest of his life. He studied hard and was an A student, which was no doubt what Ronald and Giza wanted. On his own, though, Dave read the political books that would form his worldview. He read a great deal about the Second World War. He also read about the Russian Anarchists, such as Kropotkin, who literally wrote the book on the essential organizing principle of Anarchism, *Mutual Aid*. Dave read *Brave New World*, a book which would have such an influence on him that he not only later wrote a song based on it, but would actually read aloud from the book on stage.

He also pursued his love of music. In addition to taking piano lessons, he followed all the big rock and roll bands of the time, like Led Zeppelin; Emerson, Lake & Palmer; Aerosmith; and The Rolling Stones. "But," recalls Paul Cripple (who met Dave at a third grade art show), "Dave's passion was Black Sabbath." Paul adds that Black Sabbath songs, "were never played on the three Rock stations. Maybe one song on a Sunday night while they played a Jethro Tull song every hour all week long. But Sabbath had their hardcore fans even without critics and DJs liking them."

FOUR.

In 1977, punk rock exploded onto the earth. The Sex Pistols, The Clash, The Damned, The Dead Boys, The Dictators, Iggy Pop, Johnny Thunders, and Richard Hell all released albums in 1977. The Ramones released *two* albums that year.

For Queens kids like Dave, Paul, and their buddy Russel Zanca, The Ramones were particularly important. They weren't distant rock stars from London, or even Manhattan. They had grown up in Queens, and had even attended the same high school, Forest Hills High, that Dave and Paul would soon attend. The borough of Queens would soon breed many other punks, including the members of bands like Heart Attack, Kraut, and the legendarily raw Urban Waste.

By 1978, Dave, Paul, and Russell had become punk rockers. The three of them entered ninth grade that year, a year that Russell describes as, "our coming out year as punk rockers." Like other outer borough kids, the three friends began traveling to lower Manhattan on the subway, where they could purchase punk records and clothing, and attend punk shows. Naturally, Russell says, they adopted the first wave punk uniform:

> We all got motorcycle jackets, by the time we were in high school. Dave had the first motorcycle jacket, like this little cheapie thing he got on Orchard Street in Manhattan or whatever. And he would have to go out of the house with his parka on, this down parka, and as soon as he came out of the house he'd ditch the parka in the bushes, and then he'd have his jacket on. But he couldn't let his parents know that he had his motorcycle jacket on. So that was pretty funny. Obviously for old world Jewish parents, seeing their kid with a motorcycle jacket doesn't compute.

"So were here in our last year of junior high," remembers Paul, of this time period, "And punk rock came to us. [...] So we both started a punk band called PUS." At first, the band just consisted of Dave and Paul, hashing out songs at Dave's house. In those songs were the roots of Reagan Youth songs—such as "Degenerated," "New Aryans," and "Back To The Garden Parts I- IV." "The lyrics were way different, totally politically *incorrect*," says Paul. "Definitely not what became the final product."

The original name of "Back to the Garden" was "Nipcandi," in honor of a Japanese-owned candy store, and the original name of "New Aryans" was "Planet X." For recording purposes, the band was filled out by a keyboardist named James Howard and a drummer named George, whose kit consisted of a lone snare.

When Dave and Paul entered Forest Hills High School, they met a drummer named Charles Bonet (aka Charley Tripper), who became the backbone of the group. Paul writes, "Charley looked a lot like Marky Ramone and played a lot like Tommy Ramone so he was a perfect fit." Charley in turn introduced them to a slightly older Rego Park resident named Andy Bryan (at the time he went by the name of Andy Zap, but under Dave's influence that changed to Andy Apathy). Andy was initially a guitarist, but after he switched to bass and joined Reagan Youth, the initial lineup was complete.

Andy was a bit more worldly than the other band members, who were all still in high school. "Andy was already established on the punk scene in New York city," writes Paul,

> He had somehow got himself in John Holmstrom's *Punk* magazine, and you can see him standing beside Joey Ramone and Debbie Harry in a picture where those two punk legends are supposedly getting married. Andy was credited as Andy Zap: ring bearer. [...] He was basically living the punk rock lifestyle better than we could have imagined.

The band became tighter and tighter as they practiced throughout their high school years, primarily in Russell's parents' basement. Eventually, though three of them were still in high school, they began to play shows at punk clubs in Manhattan.

FIVE.

Reagan Youth's first show—booked by Andy Apathy—was at A7, a tiny bar at the corner of Avenue A and East 7th Street that became the home of the New York City Hardcore scene. Steven Wishnia—a writer and musician who played bass in the eclectic second wave punk band False Prophets—remembers the centrality of A7 in, "Generating this scene, both the second wave of punk and the hardcore scene. A7 was crucial." Wishna explains this second wave of punk:

> Basically, by 1980, '81 the first wave of New York punk bands had pretty much all broken up. Television had broken up, The Dead Boys had broken up. The Heartbreakers had pretty much broken up by then, although they'd still do reunion gigs. The Patti Smith Group had broken up. The Contortions had broken up. The Dictators had broken up. The Ramones and Talking Heads were really it of the first wave of punk that had gotten going, and that scene had passed on to other things.
>
> The second wave was sort of all the kids and younger adults who had been outside the initial scene, but had been really inspired by it, and then went and started their own bands. So that was us, Reagan Youth, Heart Attack, The Undead, a band called Even Worse. The Stimulators were probably the first of that, with a guy named Nicky Marden. So that was us, and we were kind of doing the energy of punk, but maybe a little louder and faster.

Nicky Garratt—who was in the first wave UK band The UK Subs, and later released Reagan Youth's records on his New Red Archives label—contextualizes Dave Insurgent and Reagan Youth within this history. Garratt identifies them with two other New York punk bands of the same period: "I see them as part of the, albeit very diverse, New York triad with Kraut and the Misfits." At the same time, Dave stood out:

> Even though Reagan Youth were not at the very start of punk, Dave's songs sound as though they were conceived back then while having some of the energy of the 2nd wave. It's almost as if Dave was a first wave punk trapped in the 2nd wave.

Even as the second wave of New York punk bands were establishing themselves, a new style was evolving: Hardcore. Wishnia, whose own, diverse and experimental band never fit the hardcore mold, explains the external influences of hardcore:

> Hardcore was sort of a thing that came up from DC and LA, via Black Flag, Circle Jerks, Minor Threat. The Bad Brains sort of straddle the New York

and DC scenes because they were originally from DC, but they got their first break in New York.

SIX.

It is hard to overestimate the influence of Bad Brains on the New York Scene. Their bassist, Darryl Jennifer, wrote about the band's origins:

> Once there was a group of black teens from the Washington D.C., metro area. These teens were always on the lookout for different and new horizons in life—especially when it came to music. [...] These guys were young, black, and eclectic with their ears wide open.

As African American Rastafarians from suburban Washington D.C., The Bad Brains were unique figures in the punk world. Their speed, intensity, and positive energy were unprecedented in the history of the genre. Their background in jazz fusion meant that they actually had the musical chops to perform the music they envisioned. Their charismatic leader, H.R. (aka Human Rights, aka Paul Hudson), was a commanding presence. The arrival of Bad Brains in New York City in 1981 changed the entire direction of New York City punk rock.

The Bad Brains' self-titled first album was released in 1982. The band's live shows were already reaching a mythic status, and the recordings helped spread their influence to all corners of the punk scene, and well beyond. Greg Tate, a *Village Voice* writer who had no particular love for punk rock music, described the experience of first hearing Bad Brains:

> Now that the Brains got this 14-song cassette out on ROIR, it's for the world to know they ain't never been about no bullshitting. *Hardcore?* They take it very seriously. *You say you want hardcore?* I say the Brains'll give you hardcore coming out the ass, buddy. I'm talking about lobotomy by jackhammer, like a whirlpool bath in a concrete mixer, like orthodontic surgery by Black & Decker, like making love to a buzzsaw baby.

In New York, Bad Brains made their home at 171 A, a recording studio and rehearsal space on Avenue A. In the basement of 171 A was Dave (later Daisy) Parsons' record store, Rat Cage Records, which was a popular hangout for members of the scene. Through his DIY label (also called Rat Cage Records), Parsons released seminal records, such as The first Agnostic Front record, the first couple Beastie Boys releases, and the first Reagan Youth release, the *Youth Anthems for the New Order* EP.

The release which really captures the emergence of the second wave of New York punk rock is ROIR's 1982 compilation, *New York Thrash*. At the time, ROIR (Reach Out International Records) was a cassette-only label. This format was a perfect fit for the emerging scene. DIY punk meant using the rapidly proliferating technologies of cassette recorders and photocopiers to produce media, rather than waiting to release a vinyl LP with a major label or getting interviewed in a glossy, offset printed magazine.

Fittingly, *New York Thrash* caps off with the Stimulators classic, "Loud Fast Rules!," which, as Wishnia said, ushered in hardcore punk with its call to play louder and faster. The compilation includes two tracks from Bad Brains, as well as songs from scene stalwarts like False Prophets, Heart Attack, and Kraut. It includes tracks by lesser-remembered bands like Even Worse, and includes tracks from a band that would go to be internationally famous, The Beastie Boys. Though sometimes overlooked, the Beasties did start their career as a hardcore band (and, prior to the formation of the Beastie Boys, Adam Horovitz, aka Ad-Rock, played in the hardcore band The Young and the Useless). *New York Thrash* also includes tracks by bands from the New Jersey side of the river, Adrenaline O.D. and The Undead, the latter of which was started by Bobby Steele after he left The Misfits. The only band that is missing from the tape is Reagan Youth, though that is because Reagan Youth didn't get their shit together to contribute a track, not because ROIR wasn't interested.

SEVEN.

The first Reagan Youth recording, the *Youth Anthem For The New Order* EP would not appear until two years later, in 1984. Mike Edison—a writer, musician, editor, and former publisher of *High Times*—recalls part of why it took so long:

> I remember [Dave] putting together the first record. With the Ku Klux Klan, and See Dick Run, all that art work. "It Could Never Happen Here," that big fold out. I remember he was like pasting it together in his dorm room. It took forever. See, there was a part of Dave: I mean, I don't want to say he was a prima donna; that's not right. And I mean, how much of a perfectionist can you be if this is the medium in which you choose to work?
>
> But, I think he was like, "It's gotta be like this, it's gotta be like this, it's gotta be like this." It was a foolish unwillingness to compromise. What do you mean, compromise, Dave? Hurry up and finish your record and fucking get it out. Why, because the record company doesn't want to do an eight page foldout, giant thing? Dave, it's kind of ambitious. I know Crass does that, but just get your fucking record out so you can play California all the time and get laid and get some money so you can get better drugs, and bring your message to the people.

The ultimate goal was, very much, to get across a political message. This distinguished many of the second wave bands from the more nihilistic or apathetic first wave punk bands. Bands like Reagan Youth and False Prophets, as well as others such as Urgent Fury, No Thanks, and (A.)P.P.L.(E.)., replaced the pure nihilism of Richard Hell's *Blank Generation* with an earnest message of political resistance. Donna

Damage, the singer of No Thanks—which, like (A.)P.P.L.(E.)., was a female-fronted band in a male-dominated scene—states that her band was, "about anarchy, political activism, protest, and rebellion. We were pissed off at the world we got handed. Our motivation was to spread the word of revolution."

The influence of English anarcho-Punk bands, namely Crass (and affiliated Crass Records bands, like Zounds and Flux of Pink Indians) cannot be underestimated. London originally borrowed the idea of punk rock from New York City in the mid-seventies—The Sex Pistols were essentially a second-rate Richard Hell cover band—but London paid New York back by demonstrating that punk rock could be infused with political meaning.

Crass was an overtly anarchist band, and their anarchism went a good deal deeper than the anarchy symbol fashion statement of The Sex Pistols. In a 1981 interview with the zine *Flipside*, Crass defined what they meant by the term:

> Anarchy is the only form of political thought that does not seek to control the individual through force. Anarchy is the rejection of the State control and represents a demand by the individual to live a life of personal choice, not one of political manipulation.

Dave Insurgent was obsessed with Crass, and spoke of them constantly to his friends. Edison recalls that the artwork for the *Youth Anthem* record was heavily influenced by the packaging of the Crass records, and that Dave even aspired to have the EP released on Crass Records.

In a 1983 interview with the definitive American punk/hardcore zine, *Maximum Rocknroll (MRR)*, Dave responded to the question: "What is the anarchist message that you are trying to put across?" by saying, "It just comes down to having no authority over other people. [...] Just no authority, like governments, the church. [...] Live your life the way you want to live it." Elsewhere in the same interview, Al Pike makes it clear that what Reagan Youth was promoting was not some form of utopianism: "We don't preach political anarchy, just self anarchy." The page is illustrated with a picture of Dave—clean shaven, straight faced, and throwing up a sieg heil salute—taken by the renowned photographer Glen E. Friedman. The interview carries the tagline, "Reagan Youth, Obey the truth?"

EIGHT.

New York City has a distinct anarchist tradition that began long before the birth of punk. By the 1980s, the Lower East Side already had a history of radical political organizing stretching back a century to the days of immigrant anarchists like Johann Most, Emma Goldman, and Alexander Berkman. At the turn of the century, Jewish anarchists gathered at Sach's café on Suffolk Street to argue in Yiddish; Italian, and German anarchists gathered at other cafés and beer halls for their own debates. The anarchist movement rose to a crescendo shortly before World War I, then fractured under brutal government repression. Berkman and Goldman were deported to the newly formed Soviet Union, along with over two hundred other Russian-Jewish anarchists.

Nonetheless, the anarchist tradition continued forward. The Libertarian Book Club, which was founded in 1946, helped educate generations of Lower East Side Anarchists, along with the closely allied Libertarian League. (The term "libertarian" was not yet associated with the conservative movement, and was an understood euphemism for the dangerous term "anarchist.") The Libertarian League was founded by Sam Dolgoff and his wife, Esther. Sam had been a member of the Wobblies in the 1920s, and had been politically involved with many members of Goldman's inner circle. The Dolgoffs provided a living link to the early twentieth-century anarchist movement for the many anarchism-influenced activists who flocked to the LES in the '60s and '70s, such as the Up Against The Wall Motherfucker collective, the punks of the hippie era. The Motherfuckers were "led" by Ben Morea, a tough ex-junkie from Hell's Kitchen who wore a black leather jacket and adhered to the concept of "armed love."

The organized anarchist influence was felt by the punks of the 1980s through Anarchist Switchboard, an anarchist bookstore and community space located on East 9th street between 1st and 2nd Avenues, which was founded around 1986 by a Libertarian Book Club Member. In addition to the public space, Anarchist Switchboard's main activity was publishing a zine called *Black Eye*, which discussed classical anarchist texts, sought to relate them to contemporary situations, and offered a sweet eulogy to Esther Dolgoff when she passed away in 1988.

For the most part, though, little of the legacy of the organized political activism of the '60s and '70s remained on the Lower East Side by the early 1980s. Most groups had collapsed in the wake of the anti-war and counterculture movements. Many former activists were too burned out to be of much help to anyone; others chose to move on to more mainstream types of political involvement. In England, Crass Records was guided by older punks who had been active in the movements of the '60s. New York City's punk scene was made up of young people who largely lacked that connection, though they often searched for it.

There were only a couple holdovers from the '60s and '70s with any interest in talking to the punks on the Lower East Side. One was the Revolutionary Communist Party, a Maoist group which was (and remains) devoted to two twin goals: fomenting a communist revolution, and deifying the group's leader, a former Berkley High School football quarterback named Bob Avakian. The RCP didn't have any particular respect for the intelligence of leftist punks, but was interested in co-opting the lumpen proletariat punks, much as the British National Party co-opted the skinheads around the same time, for use as their own army. More recently, the RCP has plotted to harness the power of Occupy protestors. Avakian writes:

> While uniting with the basic and very positive thrust of the "Occupy" protests *[...] it is crucial to influence and win more and more people to seriously engage* with the scientific communist understanding and orientation—particularly as this is embodied in the outlook and strategic approach of our Party, the RCP.

The RCP has always managed to win young radicals as converts, by offering them guidance when no one else does, but there was no overwhelming desire amongst the second wave punks to ally their "basic thrust" with any "scientific communist orientation." Alec Mackaye, who played in several Washington D.C. hardcore bands around this time, writes of that scene's reaction to RCP overtures in the photobook, *Hard Art, DC 1979*: "Nobody I knew was interested in [Avakian's] plight and the RCP's vigorous pursuit of young energy started to feel desperate—like vampires in need of fresh blood."

The one other visible '60s holdover organization on the Lower East Side was the Yippies. While the term Yippie was eventually posited as an acronym for "Youth International Party," founder Abbie Hoffman defined the term as, "Energy—fun—fierceness—exclamation point!" This philosophy resonated with the punks a bit more than Avakian's program.

This '80s incarnations of the Yippies consisted not of Hoffman and Jerry Rubin, who had both moved onto other things (in Rubin's case, becoming a millionaire investor), but of various splinter groups. Former Yippies, most notably a squatter named Jerry the Peddler, were very active in the Anarchist Switchboard. This Yippie influence would continue on into subsequent anarchist infoshops, such as Sabotage Books. These infoshops (which over the years would also include A-Central, Blackout Books, and Mayday Books) provided an initial point of contact to the anarchist movement and its history for many young punks. In the late '80s, The Anarchist Switchboard would serve as a meeting and organizing space during the Tompkins Square Riots.

Another Yippie faction that remained active in New York in the '80s was a break-off group (at one point called the Zippies, for the sake of differentiation) that included figures such as Dana Beal and Aaron "the Pie Man" Kay. Dave Insurgent, who searched for connections to the '60s tradition, befriended these Yippies, and spent a good deal of time hanging out at their house on Bleecker Street. Edison remembers that one of the big draws of the Yippie scene for Dave was their May Day Pot Parade, and their general pro-marijuana stance: "Dave's big thing [was]: legalize marijuana. It really motivated him a lot. I mean, Dave loved to smoke pot. [...] Which he called busting corn." The relationship between Dave and the older radicals went a bit deeper than that, though, Edison explains:

The Yippie guys, at #9 Bleecker, there was definitely a history there. I think Dave was attracted to them. He was attracted to the '60s radicals, he had a very real connection to that. [...] He always had a sense of humor. I think he liked protests, because traditionally there's a lot of room for farce in protest movements. Abbie Hoffman was hilarious. The Yippies were pranksters. We loved the pranksters. We liked the idea of making social comment through grand performance art, and practical jokes writ large.

The Yippies' main contribution to the punk rock movement was their organization of the 1983 Rock Against Reagan tour. The tour, which was conceived as a variation of the more prominent British Rock Against Racism concerts, included political punk bands from across the country, such as Reagan Youth, MDC, The Dicks from Texas, and the Bay Area's Dead Kennedys, who were probably the most prominent political punk band of the 1980s. Mike Edison went on the tour as an opening act, performing Holocaust and Apartheid jokes in the style of an old school Borscht Belt comedian. While West Coast punk audiences loved the shows, some West Coast activists were less than impressed with the political commitment of the hard-partying New York punks.

The tour was followed up with a Rock Against Reagan concert at the protests surrounding the 1984 Democratic National Convention in San Francisco. From the Yippie perspective, this was a clear reprise of the actions surrounding the 1968 Democratic Convention in Chicago. These new punk bands were filling in for the proto-punk MC5.

As Mike Edison points out, the music of Reagan Youth and their contemporaries really was protest music. The goal was to speak truth to power. Edison contextualizes this within the tradition of Vietnam era protests:

Dave was really a hippie. That's kind of important. He was kind of a hippie-punk. And at the time, the lines were really drawn. There were peace punks, out in California, they were these guys with giant spikes, but they were fucking hippies. I mean, they played fast, and aggressively. Bands like MDC, but there were a lot of other bands as well.

EIGHT.

"Not only was Reagan Youth great," says Nicky Garratt, in Steven Blush's oral history, *American Hardcore*. "They really stood for something. In the days of Reagan, it was really important for there to be a band who expressed all the pain, anguish, and alienation kids were feeling."

It goes almost without saying that Reagan Youth was a product of the age of Reagan. Their name is an ironic reference to the Hitler Youth. If anything, Reagan Youth and their contemporaries emulated the Swing Kids, the German teenage rebels who danced to jazz instead of doing their Hitlerjugend (Hitler Youth) service, or the White Rose, who distributed anti-Hitler leaflets and painted anti-Hitler graffiti. As tongue and cheek as the Reaganism-as-Nazism satire was (Dave was a Jewish comedian, as much as he was anything), it was at least as earnest as it was hyperbolic. "He was earnest," says Edison. "When he said 'I hate hate' or 'liberate yourself' or 'Fuck Reagan,' he meant it. These were the battle cries of our time." And, as Edison explains, these were dire times indeed:

> Reagan was destroying the Middle Class, and dividing Rich and Poor, Black and White, and polarizing the country. We were feeling that the country was heading in the wrong direction. It was pretty earnest. It seemed like there was a war looming.

Reagan Youth's eponymous anthem includes the lyrics: "Want another war? Forward to El Salvador. Gonna kill some communists!" Though it is largely forgotten by the American public, throughout the 1980s a brutal civil war ravaged El Salvador, ultimately leaving over 70,000 people dead.

Urgent Fury's band name referenced another overlooked conflict in the Americas: Reagan's internationally condemned 1983 invasion of the sovereign Caribbean nation of Grenada. In their song, "58,000 Dead," Urgent Fury compares the growing U.S. involvement in El Salvador to the U.S. experience in Vietnam. "Let's see if you remember," their singer, Abraham Rodriguez, demanded, referencing the 58,000 American servicemen killed in a senseless war. In a 1988 interview with the British zine *Artcore*, Rodriguez (who went on to become an acclaimed novelist), explained the motivations behind the song:

> I relate to veterans from 'Nam, some of which lived on my street like beggars, they went through heavy shit and this is the thanks they get! So I scribbled "58,000 dead" one day after hours with my guitar.

It didn't seem like anyone did remember Vietnam, though. Vietnam veterans roamed the streets of America's cities; rather than funding domestic programs to help these Americans in need, Reagan gave millions of dollars in military aid to the rightist Salvadoran government, whose tactics for combating communist dissidents including clandestine hit squads, and the bombing of civilian villages. Reagan's regime came to power only five years after the fall of Saigon, but the U.S. government was more than happy to plunge headlong into another brutal war against the specter of communism. American society, as a whole, seemed oblivious.

The cover of *Reagan Youth: Volume 1* features a Ku Klux Klan member patting a smiling child on the head. Beneath the photo are the words: "Oh come on now Jim, it could never happen here." The point was that—as Sinclair Lewis made clear in his 1935 novel, *It Can't Happen Here*—of course fascism could, and does, occur in America.

African American and Latino neighborhoods in New York and other U.S. cities suffered terrible violence and degradation in the 1980s, as Reagan cut social programs, the industrial base of U.S. cities continued to erode, and the crack epidemic exploded (largely as a result of another of Reagan's anti-communist adventures in Latin American, in this case in Nicaragua). Gay men were dying from AIDS in epidemic numbers, while Reagan's Christian Right supporters claimed that this was God's judgment.

Another Reagan Youth song that fits in with their titular conceit is "New Aryans." "Be proud that you're a white American," the song begins. The sarcasm drops away, and by the middle of the song Dave is singing, "Death to the Nazis and the Ku Klux Klan/ Anarchy in the Fatherland." As the son of Holocaust survivors, Dave was more viscerally conscious of the actual trauma associated with Nazi symbols than the many other punks of the day (like the Dead Kennedys) who also used Nazi imagery ironically. Wishnia—whose own grandparents lost many of their family members in the Holocaust—sums up the message Dave sent by using the name Reagan Youth: "This is what my parents went through, and I'm scared I'm going to have to go through it."

NINE.

The "hippie values" of Insurgent and other like-minded punks were not solely a response to the Reagan Regime. These values—as conflicting and unspecific as they often were—included not just political protest and societal liberation, but spiritual growth and personal liberation. The second wave punks had inherited the energy and rebellion of the original punks, but they were interested in attempting to create a culture with enough support, depth, and positivity to nourish and sustain its participants. For better or worse, these new punks wanted a truly meaningful punk experience. They wanted a punk rock that could save them.

Gee Vaucher, a visual artist whose work defined the aesthetic of Crass, describes the larger, more metaphysical questions that build from the foundation of anarcho-punk values in a recent interview:

> It's all about sensitivity, it's all about truth, honesty, understanding the foundation of the problem. How far do you go back? Do you just stem the wound with a plaster or do you go back further and see what's creating it? It's the same with your health. It's holistic. Because life is holistic isn't it? You can't just take one little bit. Everything to me is so linked. You have to step back and see where it all comes from... it's unending

The Dead Kennedys song, "Nazi Punks Fuck Off," begins with the line, "Punk ain't no religious cult." The point of the song is to call to task the anti-intellectual thugs of the hardcore scene of the day, and implore punks to think for themselves.

While this is a laudable message, the fact of the matter is that punk essentially is a leaderless religious cult.

Punks, as a whole, have always been opposed to the hypocrisy and social control of organized religion, particularly the dominant American Christian institutions. An example of that is the Reagan Youth song, "In Dog We Trust." At the same time, other Reagan Youth songs, like "One Holy Bible," seem to be searching for some spiritual truth that exists outside of the confines of organized religion. "Dave was trying to find himself spiritually," says Edison. "He dropped a lot of acid. We were trying to find answers, like anybody else." Dave's former girlfriend, Susan, echoes this sentiment: "Dave had a desire to touch the infinite, or transcend. He was a young twenty-something seeker grappling with the big questions of life."

Insurgent was by no means alone in this quest. In his memoir, *The Evolution of a Cro-Magnon*, John Joseph—a Hare Krishna devotee, AWOL sailor, and former Bad Brains roadie—discussed a collective attempt to grapple with the larger questions of life:

> H.R. and I started an organization called the "United Freedom Fighters," or U.F.F. We had a few meetings, which included the late singer of Reagan Youth, Dave Insurgent, and a bunch of other dudes who played in bands. We sat around and talked about God, philosophy, and revolution against the Babylon system. To H.R., the youth were everything. As Bob Marley said in one of his songs, "The Babylon System is the vampire, sucking on the blood of the children day by day." We talked about doing benefit concerts, taking trips to Africa, organizing martial arts classes and shutting down slaughterhouses and abortion clinics in the U.S.

It should be pointed out that shutting down abortion clinics is a horrible goal. Using force to deny women autonomy over their own bodies is one of the least anarchist sentiments imaginable. The passage reflects Joseph's own views, and clearly not everyone in a group of punks was agreeing with each other on everything. The sentiment does, however, reflect the growing macho stance of the hardcore scene. It also reflects the influence of H.R. Many in the scene looked up to H.R. as a role model, and as a benchmark of authenticity. The Bad Brains' drift into Rastafarianism is probably what opened the door for religiosity in the punk scene to begin with. As H.R. got deeper into conservative Rastafarianism (not to mention drugs and mental illness), he became more known for homophobia and misogyny than for positivity.

The U.F.F. story is interesting though, because it shows a conscious attempt by members of Bad Brains, Cro-Mags, Reagan Youth, and others to articulate a clear scene vision of spiritual and political growth. Even the most macho and apolitical hardcore bands were drawn to spiritual ideas. The most overt example of this was the Cro-Mags, a band that included Joseph and Harley Flanagan (who, though still a young teenager, was already a scene veteran, having played drums with The Stimulators at the age of thirteen). The Cro-Mags were very much a Hare Krishna band, in the way that Reagan Youth was an anarchist band. The title of their first record, *Age of Quarrel*, is a reference to the Hindu concept of Kali Yaga, and over the years John Joseph would be as much known for his involvement in the Hare Krishna movement as his involvement in the hardcore scene.

The Krishna movement had a widespread appeal in the hardcore scene. Its values of spiritual transcendence appealed to the kids' search for meaning, but its austerity and self-denial allowed for a tough-guy stance that countered any whiff of hippie or weakness. What's more, the movement was born on the same Lower East Side streets as punk rock itself, in the mid-sixties, when A. C. Bhaktivedanta Swami Prabhupada arrived from India to preach his own vision of Hinduism to the west. Prabhupada's movement (incorporated as the International Society for Krishna Consciousness) soon gained followers, who praised it for making the wisdom of the Vedas accessible to Americans. At the same time, the movement gained many critics, who justifiably characterized the movement as a cult, whose leaders exploited naïve young spiritual seekers for their own benefit.

Cro-Mags were far from the only punks interested in Hare Krishna. Many, including Dave Insurgent, dabbled in it, without developing a lasting connection, while others took it much more seriously. Ray Cappo and Porcell were members of Youth of Today, a hardcore band from Connecticut that was involved in the New York hardcore scene in the latter half of the eighties. At the end of that decade, Cappo and Porcell went on to form Shelter, an influential and overtly Krishna band. Cappo also founded Equal Vision Records, an Albany-based record label dedicated to promoting the emerging "Krishnacore" scene.

TEN.

By the middle of the eighties, bands like Cro-Mags had come to dominate the New York scene. By now, it was decidedly a "hardcore" scene, not a "punk" scene, and the youth crews that flocked to the CBGB matinees were more interested in starting their own street fights than in protesting Reagan's wars. While the Cro-Mags' Krishna vision may not have been wildly popular, their lifestyle of vegetarianism, working out, and starting fist fights certainly was. What this meant was that the positive peace punks were being muscled out of their own scene. Steven Blush describes the shift in his book:

> By '84 New York Hardcore had changed, shifting from a somewhat Left-Wing scene to a violent Skinhead stance led by Cro-Mags, Murphy's Law, Agnostic Front, and Cause for Alarm. [...] It was as if all the smart people were being driven out—definitely ending the first wave.

Today, the term "New York Hardcore" (or NYHC) conjures images of this later scene, which came to be dominated by the tough-guy, skinhead style. Associated primarily with Agnostic Front, as well as other bands such as Cro-Mags and Warzone (all three of whom made great early records, to be fair), this skinhead hardcore style was centered around unity and street violence, and left little room for free thought or individuality. Abraham Rodriguez looked back at this period, in a column for the German zine *Oxblood*:

> The bands that REALLY were 'political' were shunted to the side and relegated to the ghetto that came to be known as "the peace punk scene." And such excellent bands as VIRUS, HEART ATTACK, and REAGAN YOUTH are mostly by-passed to give kudos to the big monster that ate it all: AGNOSTIC FRONT, which, hate to tell you, at the time, was an apolitical reactionary band which encouraged if not fostered the rise of a skinhead movement that was the bane of every band trying to say something about what was going on. Mind you, one of the interesting things about AGGIE FRONT was how actually vague they were politically; in other words, to call them 'rightist' would be a big mistake. This band espoused no political beliefs that one could pin down. They hated the system all right. They hated everything, especially peace punks.

The term "skinhead," in this context, refers only to the specific to the skinhead strain within the New York Hardcore scene. "Skinhead" in of itself can mean almost as many different things as "punk" can. Skinhead has a long and complex history, dating back to the multi-racial working class youth culture that developed in 1960s England, which was steeped in Jamaican music, and is still upheld by traditional (trad) skinheads. The White Power co-option of the subculture that began in 1970s England certainly spilled over into America in the late '80s, gaining a foothold in American cities such as Portland and Minneapolis.

Craig Flanigan, who, before starting God Is My Co-Pilot, was one of the original New York City SHARP (Skinheads Against Racial Prejudice) recalls that there were battles within New York Skinhead over the direction the scene would take:

> There were a lot of people who picked up the British style of dressing, and music, and aggro, which was pretty well-suited to New York in the early '80s. It wasn't really a pose, or a pretention. Some of the other people who picked it up, what happened was there were actually recruiters from DASH and CASH—which were Detroit Area Skinheads and Chicago Area Skinheads, which were rightwing groups with money behind them. Everyone I knew said the money was from the Klan, but who the hell actually knows. But they had money, and they had people flying them to New York to politicize

skinheads in a right-wing way. And that's when BASH—Brooklyn Area Skinheads—started.

At that point my friend Marcus said, "Something must be done. There is SHARP. There are Trojan Skins, and the old spirit of '67 in London, and we have to have that here. I said, "Oh. OK, sure." He asked a bunch of people to do it, and a lot of people were scared. But Troy was never scared of anything, and I had never had much sense, so we started this thing.

With the increased media attention on skinhead, more young, violent, and nationalist skinheads would be attracted to the scene. Groups of thugs emerged, such as the notorious DMS crew. At the same time, others crews, such as RASH (Red and Anarchist Skinheads) came together to attempt to define skinhead as a positive youth movement, in the vein of punk. And, ultimately, the multi-racial nature of the New York Skinhead scene—there were always plenty of Latino skinheads in New York—meant that a white supremacist ideology would never be entirely welcome in that scene, even if other nationalist and rightist ideologies would be.

Indeed, Esneider, of the Hispanophone New York band Huasipungo, observed one of the complexities of the split between the scenes in *Maximumrocknroll*: "the anarcho-punk and/or hardcore punk scene was mostly white, while the violent, homophobic skin scene was actually anti-racist and very diverse." Agnostic Front's lead singer, Roger Miret, for example, was born in Cuba. In *American Hardcore*, he describes his relationship to the largely-Latino Lower East Side: "There were lots of gangs. It was a very Hispanic hood. I'm Hispanic, so I was the in-between man talking to these people." It may be worth considering that Dave Insurgent was not the only one bringing his family experience with him into the scene. Perhaps Agnostic Front would not have been so hostile to left-wing punks if Miret himself were not a refugee from a Communist regime.

Undeniably, though, the skinhead strain in the '80s hardcore scene was emblematic of a shift towards violence and intolerance. Flanigan recalls:

> There were a lot of gay skinheads in the early and mid '80s. None of them were wearing pink triangles under their American flags, but it was also no big secret until the whole Nazi thing came along. [...] There was no real prevalent anti-gay rhetoric, and no real violent homophobia, that I ever saw in punk rock from 1979 to 1985. It was just pretty inclusive.

But then things changed. In a 2007 webzine interview, Donna Damage recounted:

> Hardcore Punk was the place for the kids from my generation to go that accepted you for what you were. This is where the thinkers went. This is where the kids who shopped at thrift stores and put together their own style. Kids who read books. Kids who hated the government and Ronnie Reagan. HC was a rebellion. I stopped participating when kids got hurt for not being

in uniform. I was done with it, the night I watched a tranny guy get his brains stomped out in Tompkins Square by some later to be rock star skins and their followers.

The violent hate crime that Donna describes was by no means an isolated incident. John Joseph describes the activities of his own band mates:

> The Cro-Mags at that point had a Nazi skinhead reputation because Harley and Eric dressed like skins. Harley got a swastika tattoo and they engaged in gay bashing with the other knucklehead skinheads they hung out with. [...] Harley and Eric made the front cover of this big gay magazine that had a picture of them about to fuck someone up. The caption read, "GENTLEMAN... BEWARE OF THESE TWO SKINHEADS."

The Reagan Youth joke started to seem less funny when people in the same scene were actually acting like Brown Shirts. Dave Insurgent's reaction to the skinheads was to go the other way: he grew his hair out into long dreadlocks (like his hero, H.R.), and even began wearing tie-dye and shorts. Dave's girlfriend, Susan, made tie-dye t-shirts to sell as band merchandise at shows, which proved to be more profitable than the gigs themselves. "It was quite funny," she recalls, "To see the punk rockers in pink RY tie-dyes from the batch that had the red dye mixed too strong."

Reagan Youth also began to break every rule of punk by playing Grateful Dead covers live. The band—which now included Javier Madriaga (aka Johnny Aztec), who also played drums in (A.)P.P.L.(E.)—would also smoke pot on stage, and play extended covers of Black Sabbath's anti-war song, "War Pigs." Paul recalls that, "Dave really wanted us to cover 'If Six Was Nine' by Hendrix so he could change the line 'If all the hippies cut off all their hair' to 'If all the skinheads grew out all their hair.'" In a 1987 interview with the zine *Bad Newz*, Dave discusses the rift in the scene:

> It's about accepting other's freedoms. That's what we're into. And I hear Agnostic Front say it, I hear the Cro-Mags say it. Hopefully everyone's sayin' the same thing—unity-unity-unity—but I hope they mean it.

"After the mid-80s," says Russell Zanca:

> I don't really have a sense that David even thought that there was a chance for a really coherent movement, that it would go more political or something like that. I think it was more like, he felt he wanted to be that kind of person, and that's where he wanted to take Reagan Youth, and if there was a circle of people around him that felt very similarly, and there was a few bands around him that had that kind of ethos, he was good with that.

In the *Artcore* interview, Rodriguez expresses a similar sentiment:

> We have refused to play shows with bands we felt would make us look like hypocrites, bands who didn't think about things like racism, sexism, violence. We want nothing to do with that shit, we're not a scene, we're Urgent Fury

> and we want people to come see us without getting their heads kicked in by goons.

For bands like Reagan Youth and Urgent Fury, who had been around in the early '80s, the shift in the scene felt like a betrayal. The originators of both scenes had played shows together at A7 and CBGB, after all. By the late '80s, though, younger punks and skins did not even consider themselves part of the same scene. Skinheads came to punk shows with the intention of disrupting them and causing violence, and gang style fights would break out between the two groups. Fly, an artist, musician, and activist, recalls that, "These were serious fucking fights." Spike Polite, front man of the street punk band Sewage, clarifies Fly's statement: "I mean like broken bones, and people getting stabbed up." Sascha Altman DuBrul, a writer, activist, and bass player of the band Choking Victim who became involved in the punk scene as a young teenager in the late '80s, recalls the resulting cultural division:

> In high school I was a young punk rocker and one of my best friends was a young skinhead. Then I started hanging with the anarchist punks on the LES and he started hanging with his crew of older skinheads that liked to fight and be boneheads. We would see each other in our respective crews walking through Tompkins, and eye each other warily, not acknowledge one another.

ELEVEN.

The violence of skinheads paled in comparison to the violence of a more organized and more destructive group that was increasingly present on the Lower East Side in the late 1980s: The New York City Police Department (NYPD).

In previous decades, the police presence on the Lower East Side had been fairly minimal. Due to factors such as white flight, industrial decline, and governmental neglect, the area had become completely disinvested. The municipal government was facing severe financial problems, and had no interest in using its limited resources to provide adequate police, firefighting, or sanitation services to an area that was predominately low-income and Latino. The area became noted for burned-out and collapsing tenements, and an economy dominated by drug sales.

It is important to note that, despite these conditions, the Lower East Side was home to a culturally thriving New York Puerto Rican (Nuyorican) community. Internal immigrants had begun to arrive in New York City from Puerto Rico in large numbers in the 1940s and '50s, just as Jews (and other white ethnic immigrant groups, such as Ukrainians) were beginning to abandon the slum conditions of the Lower East Side for the outer boroughs and suburbs. Puerto Ricans moved into the shifting neighborhood in large numbers, rechristening it Loisaida.

By the mid-1970s, the squatter and community garden movements began to arise as grassroots responses to the situation in the neighborhood. Empty buildings were turned into homes, and empty lots were turned into gardens. These movements were never fully cohesive, by any means. Some squatters were people from the neighborhood, who were simply interested in securing housing for their families. Some squatters—such as the group CHARAS, which occupied an abandoned public high school—were organized Latino community activists. Other squatters were ideological Marxists or Anarchists, with strong ideas about collective living and collective action. A group of people coming together to contribute their own skills, and autonomously provide housing, is a practical expression of Kropotkin's core anarchist concept of Mutual Aid. Other squatters were punk rockers and artists, who were looking for a way to sustain their lives and art without compromise. As Fly, who was and is an active member of the squatter movement, recalls:

> A lot of people squatted for convenience. That was fine too, if they put in their work days. Some people weren't into putting in work days; they wanted to squat so they could do a lot of drugs, and not pay rent. But the core of the squatter movement in the Lower East Side was pretty huge, in the '80s and '90s.

Eventually, Fly says, "Squatting on the Lower East Side became a cohesive community as a political movement."

Parallel to the growth of squatting as a cohesive political community, a squatter punk culture emerged. This is not to say that all squatters were interested in punk rock music. There were plenty of squatters who were involved in the noise, jazz, and improv scenes. The late Michael Shenker, an activist, musician, and electrician who helped generations of squatters hook up their electricity, even worked on a squatter opera, which was produced as a work in progress at the Living Theatre in 1994. Still, the squats were a magnet for punk kids and punk bands. DuBrul recalls the scene in the late '80s:

> There was a whole bunch of squatter punk kids. There were buildings that were filled with young, punk-identified squatters. There was C-Squat, and Pest Squat, there was 3BC, and Fetus Squat.

These squats provided not just places for punks to live, but places for punk bands to practice and perform. DuBrul continues:

> Neil and Ralphy Boy were doing these Squat or Rot shows, which happened at a few different squats, on the ground floor, or in the backyard, or in the basement.

In addition to the Squat or Rot shows, there were plenty of other punk shows held at various squatted buildings. Some shows took place at The Gas Station, an actual former gas station which had been taken over by The Rivington School, a collective of welder/artists. These squat shows meant that punk bands were no longer dependent on club owners to book shows, but could organize shows on their own terms. The audiences for these shows tended to be drawn from the large population of punks who lived or hung out in the neighborhood on a daily basis. They did not attract the broad audiences that more mainstream punk shows would start to attract in the mid-'90s. At the time, DuBrul recalls, "The people who were getting into punk tended to be people who were just more alienated and fucked-up."

Whatever their cultural affiliation, or personal or political motivation, all the squatters, community gardeners, and community activists came to face a common threat. By the mid-1980s, the gentrification of lower Manhattan was gearing up. The section of the Lower East Side above Houston Street—which includes Alphabet City, and was by now known as the East Village—became hip and desirable. The presence of white artists and musicians certainly helped to precipitate this shift, but all Manhattan real estate was being gobbled up by gentrification, and the economic disparity between the Lower East Side and other areas made it vulnerable to speculators and developers.

The blocks that had been completely neglected by the city for decades were suddenly valuable properties. Very quickly, rents began to double and triple. The police had never cared when junkies died on the Lower East Side, but in 1984 a huge effort was put into clearing drug dealers and users off the street, in the form of a massive police attack known as Operation Pressure Point, which was personally led by Mayor Ed Koch.

The city also began to collude with developers to drive out the squatters, the gardeners, the elderly and Latino residents of rent-controlled apartments, and anyone else who couldn't pay rising market rates for housing. A violent effort by the city to drive out squatters persisted throughout the early '90s, coming to a head with the 1995 eviction of the 13th Street squats. During these evictions, the city laid siege to the buildings with military force, including, according to the National Housing Institute, "officers in riot gear, helicopters, a tank, and a sniper."

Still, some of the resistance was successful, and a small amount of buildings that were squatted in the 1980s remain in the hands of their residents. In 2002, eleven former squats—including the notoriously punk rock C-Squat, home to members of crusty punk bands such as Leftover Crack, Morning Glory, and Nausea—were recognized by the city as legal limited-equity co-ops, and residents were able to begin the process of purchasing their homes through the Urban Homesteading Assistance Board.

Another squatted building which was eventually legally recognized after a hard fight is ABC No RIO, an anarchist arts and activism space on Rivington Street. ABC was originally opened up by an earlier generation of anarchists and artists in 1980, but in the early '90s there was a shift, and the punks took over. ABC has been home to many different types of performance series, but it is primarily known for the weekly Saturday hardcore/punk matinees, which began in 1990, and have been going on ever since. The ABC matinees were very consciously started as an alternative to the violent and exclusionary CBGB matinees, and have always had a firm policy of not allowing racist, sexist, or homophobic bands or behavior. In an oral history of ABC no Rio, original matinee booker Mike Bullshit recalled his motivation in enforcing the policy: "I'm gay and I'm booking the shows. And if you hate gays and think they're doing something wrong, then you shouldn't play here." ABC is still going strong, and is currently beginning a massive rebuilding process. Long after CBGB closed down, and was replaced with a boutique specializing in expensive "punky" clothing, ABC continues to hold weekly, all-ages matinees, with zero tolerance for prejudice and violence.

TWELVE.

The most fiercely contested space in the history of the Lower East Side is Tompkins Square Park. Nestled between Avenues A and B, and E. 7th and E. 10th Streets, Tompkins had been the social, cultural, and political heart of the Lower East Side for over 150 years, since the days when German and Irish shipyard workers would gather there to protest unemployment and the draft. It was the heart of the '60s and '70s Lower East Side counter culture, and in the '80s it was a gathering place for punks and squatters, as well as home to many people considered homeless.

When the police tried to implement a 1 AM curfew in the park on August 6, 1988, the locals and activists gathered to resist. Journalist Sarah Ferguson writes:

> Activists, squatters among them, saw the curfew as another effort to tame the Lower East Side for a wealthier class of people. The militants were apoplectic. This was an invasion of their turf, an effort by the police and real estate developers to assert control over the "people's" park, to remake its rough, unsocialized edges into something more akin to Union Square.

The activists were ready for a fight, but the NYPD's invasion of the park was more violent than expected. The message was clear: the city would use any amount of force to colonize the LES for yuppie development. Even the *New York Times* admitted the military nature of the invasion of the park:

> Hundreds of demonstrators protesting the overnight closing of a park in Manhattan's East Village clashed with 450 riot-equipped police officers early yesterday in bloody street skirmishes that turned the neighborhood into something like a war zone.

The NYPD had not expected the level of resistance they would face from activists, nor the bad press that their own violence would generate. In the wake of the '88 riots, homeless people and activists moved in, completely occupying the park. This set the stage for further conflict with the police. DuBrul, who participated in the riots as a high school student, recalls the situation the following year:

> In '89, what went down was basically that there were all these homeless folks that had created a tent village in Tomkins Square Park, and the city wanted to kick them out. Tompkins Square Park was kind of a scary place to hang out. In the wintertime, people would chop up the benches and burn them. It was a wild place.

When the police attempted to evict the tent city, they were once again met with fierce resistance, which made a strong impact on the young DuBrul:

> When I walk down St. Marks Place and reach Avenue A, the entrance to the park right there, I see what's going on there, I'm cognizant of what's going on there now, but I always flash back to when there was an enormous bonfire in the street made of police barricades, and there were people standing around it, screaming and shouting. And the police were running. It was beautiful. It definitely felt like solidarity.

Conflict over the space would continue over the next two years. Fly, who participated in the riots, describes the attitude of the NYPD at the time:

> After the '88 riot, they were so humiliated by the horrible press that they got—well deserved horrible press—that they wanted to up the ante. They didn't want to fuck around anymore.

The police repeatedly confronted the park inhabitants and activists with militarized displays of force, physical violence, and unsubstantiated arrests and charges. Many of these arrests came days after the riots, when protestors were tracked down at their homes using identifications based on police surveillance and media footage. In a few cases, rioters were even charged with terrorism, prefiguring an anti-dissent tactic which would become more widely used in the 2000s, following 9/11.

During the riots, punks and activists directly confronted the police violence, using everything from their own hands to stones, firecrackers, fruits and vegetables, bottles, and even occasionally Molotov cocktails. Fly recalls that, "People were going to the recycling center and getting the bottles." Police barricades were countered with bonfires. Trumped up charges were challenged in court by activist lawyers.

Meanwhile, park-life thrived. People continued to inhabit the tent city, punks and squatters continued to hang out in the park, and shows continued to be held in the park, with bands playing in the park's stone band shell. Tent city residents, squatters, and punks from around the city and suburbs would come out to the shows.

Most of the bands playing in the band shell were, of course, punk bands. One of the few live videos that exists of Dave Insurgent singing with Reagan Youth was shot there. Perhaps the most notorious band to play in the park, though, was the industrial group, Missing Foundation. The band's leader, Peter Missing, helped define the visual aesthetic of the Tompkins Square riots, with his ubiquitous "1988=1933" and upside martini glass emblem graffiti. DuBrul recalls:

> Back in those days there was one of those upside down martini glasses on every block. Pete Missing tagged every block. They weren't even really a band. They were like a cultural phenomenon. The police were scared of them. They would play in Tompkins Square Park, the police wouldn't come in the park.

During these years, punk shows in the park frequently led to police confrontation. These were legal, permitted shows, but the NYPD was not particularly concerned with legality. A particular occasion of conflict was the annual Squatter May Day shows. Spike Polite recalls the confrontation that occurred between punks and police at the 1991 May Day show:

> We were leaving because they shut the show down early, because they didn't want people playing no music there in memory of a riot where they were beating people up. The cops were acting rude to everyone in the audience, who were sticking around and hovering. The cops just started grabbing people.

One of the people grabbed was a friend of Spike's named Rodney, an African-American punk who was viciously beaten and arrested for the crime of carrying an unopened beer into the park. This led to a confrontation between the police and the punks, who, after nearly pulling Rodney apart, managed to unarrest him. "The cops were pissed," recalls Spike, "But they couldn't do nothing, because the people started rushing in." Eventually, the outnumbered police got back into their cars and retreated. One cop got left behind:

> Everybody followed this other cop that came up on foot, and we chased him through the park. He was running to get away from us now. We had just seen what the cops were doing, and other people were saying some other incidents like this had happened throughout the day. So we're like, fuck it, they're going to arrest everybody anyway, so let's get this little guy. You know, like he's a cockroach and you found him in your fridge. Kill him. Squash him. So we chased him down the middle of the park, and then Ninth Street. We got around to the other side, and we caught up with him. More people—disgruntled concert goers—came out and trapped him off.
>
> Cops were coming to save him, because as he was running, he was talking on his walkie-talkie. But everybody ran up, and we just grabbed him. Usually in the punk rock thing, in England, you take the badge off the officer and you wear it on your jacket upside down. But he got stripped. We took his gun, his radio, someone got his wallet [...] We were like, "We're gonna fucking kill you, raaaaahhhhhh!" He's like, "Ahhhh, don't kill me, I got a wife

and family." And we're like, "You should have thought of that before you were beating on innocent people."

Such victories were short-lived. Less than a month later, on May 27, 1991, the final confrontation came in the form of the Memorial Day Riot. This riot started the same way as the May Day Riot: with the police shutting down a show. The police and the rioters battled on Avenue A. Unfortunately, the focus of resistance was lost, and some rioters looted a local mom and pop store. As DuBrul observes, the problem with riots is that, "people aren't thinking about what they're doing."

The senseless attack on a small, immigrant-owned business was a blow to the perception of the riots, and was just the sort of excuse the city was looking for—not that they needed one. In the weeks following the Memorial Day Riot, the park was completely closed to the public by the Dinkins administration, ostensibly for needed renovation. Fly recalls that, for over a year, "The whole way around the park was just police and barricades." A key element of the renovation of the park was the destruction of the stone band shell, where so many bands had played. What was happening was bigger than the punks, though. "Whatever we were doing," says DuBrul, "it had a lot more to do with real estate, and the shifting tide of New York. They closed the park down, and clearly they were strategizing. They put a bunch of money into renovating it, and when it opened back up, it wasn't a place to hang out. The era was dying."

The government's occupation and renovation of the park was not without precedent; the city had used similar tactics following the protests by shipyard workers in the late 1800s. This time, though, the changes in the park were part of larger, more permanent shifts. The Lower East Side environment that fostered the second wave punk scene was completely lost to gentrification by the mid-nineties. The Dinkins administration was succeeded by the Giuliani administration, which was characterized by unprecedented levels of social control, militarized policing, and privatization of the city. To younger anarcho-punks, the 1988-91 riots stand as a legendary pinnacle of resistance. In reality, it was a death knell. As Ferguson writes:

> The squatting and political movements that rose up in and around Tompkins Square from roughly 1985 to 1995 was in many ways the last generation of activists to conceive of the Lower East Side as an oppositional space.

THIRTEEN.

By 1995, Dave Insurgent, the archetypical Lower East Side anarcho-punk, was dead.

Reagan Youth officially broke up in 1988, when Ronald Reagan ended his second term in office. That same year, the Berlin Wall fell, and the entire political alignment of the world shifted. The Reagan Regime continued on with Reagan's Vice

President, George H. Bush, in power, but the historical moment was over, and the damage was done.

Dave and Paul attempted to start a new project, House of God, which went in a dramatically different direction than Reagan Youth. Paul describes the intent of the project:

> The music had become more complex, but it would still remain catchy as hell. So instead of two minute political punk rock songs, we were going to play 8 minute songs about the evils of organized religion.

For the most part, punk audiences were more confused than excited about the new band's performances.

The main reason that House of God never got off the ground was not the punk scene's lack of acceptance for creative projects, but Dave's own escalating drug addiction. He had always been an enthusiastic recreational user of various drugs, not to mention a pot dealer, but by the late '80s he had descended into the heroin addiction that would dominate the rest of his life. "Dave was just going deeper and deeper into this abyss he couldn't get out of," says Russell. "By like '87, '88, every time I talked to him, it's just like, wow, he's going down. He's kind of losing his mental integrity." Susan and Dave—who had been living together for years at this point—broke up. "After I left," she recalls, "He called one day freaked out that he had woken up in a crack house. Part of him knew that what he was doing was scary and could have consequences."

Reagan Youth's *Volume 1* was not released until later in 1989, after the band had broken up, and *Volume 2* was not released until the following year. *Volume 1* is a punk classic, and contains all of Reagan Youth's most beloved songs. That being said, it was not a new record; it consists of re-mastered versions of the seven tracks from the *Youth Anthems* EP, as well as the three tracks cut from the original EP. Essentially, *Volume 1* is the great, first Reagan Youth album, that should have come out five years earlier, when the songs were recorded at Reagan Youth's height.

Volume 2 to some degree reflects a different, less decidedly punk style. As Paul explains, though, these songs were still a part of the integral Reagan Youth experience:

> Songs such as "Back To Garden", "One Holy Bible" and "Queen Babylon" were around since 1980, with the original lineup. I know it sounds like we were taking the band in a new direction but that was not the case. Those songs, though longer and with more complex arrangements, are definitely Reagan Youth 'type' songs. And every song we recorded was played live at one time or another between 1981-1989.

The records were recorded and released by Nicky Garratt's New Red Archives, which was, at that point a fledging New York City label (it would later move to San Francisco, its current home). Garratt recalls the difficulty of working with Dave, in the condition that he was in in 1989:

> It wasn't hard working with Dave, what was hard was trespassing on his drug life. Paul and I had to ostensibly kidnap him to do the vocals on volume 2 and we didn't let him out until he'd finished.
>
> Here's the start of a letter I wrote to Dave dated 15th Jan 1990:
>
> Please call me immediately
>
> I have no working phone # for you. Your beeper # is now someone called 'Charlie' and your original # is no good. I have been sitting on these test cuts for days now, if I don't hear from you by tomorrow I will approve them myself (they are pretty much as you mixed them). Etc. etc.

Before the final touches on *Volume 2* were completed, Dave was viciously beaten with a baseball bat by a drug dealer, whom he owed money to. The brain trauma was so severe that a lobotomy was required. Dave lived with his parents in Queens while he recuperated, but it was only a matter of time before he was back on the Lower East Side, strung out.

During the last few years of Dave Insurgent's life, his heroin addiction obscured and precluded everything else. Heroin addiction has taken a greater toll

on punks and punk scenes than any other force. As Garratt says of Dave: "His freewheeling lyrics and song style should be celebrated while his addictions frowned upon and pitied. Certainly there is nothing glamorous about his decline."

In 1993, Dave was dating a twenty-two year old aspiring dancer from Louisiana named Tiffany Bresciani, who was also addicted to heroin. On June 24, 1993, Tiffany and Dave went down to Allen Street on the Lower East Side, so Tiffany could turn a trick to get money for Dave and her to cop dope. She went off with a customer and never came back. Four days later, her corpse was found in the back of serial killer Joel Rifkin's truck on Long Island.

Two days after that, on June 30, 1993, Dave's Holocaust-survivor mother, Giza, was killed in a freak accident involving a car driven by Dave's father at their home in Queens.

Three days later, on July 3, 1993, Dave Insurgent killed himself. He was twenty-nine years old. Ronald Rubinstein, who had survived Stalin's gulag, and marched into Tehran with General Anders, was forced to bury his wife and son during the same week.

"He was my mentor, my band mate, and my friend," Paul Cripple said of Dave. "He failed me in all that."

FOURTEEN.

Russell Zanca remembers that, most of all, Dave "loved the opportunity to be onstage with a microphone and talk to people. I can't stress that strongly enough." Some examples of Dave doing just that were captured on tape, and released on the *Live & Rare* compilation five years after his death.

The first track on *Live & Rare* is the song, "Beautiful Day." A highlight of the Reagan Youth stage show was the lengthy intro Dave would perform for the song, which describes a group of apathetic Americans who are wasting away a day having a barbeque, enjoying their beers and hotdogs, when a war begins and missiles began to land and explode in America.

In the last moments of calm, before the "first bombs start dropping," and Paul's guitar starts wailing like an air-raid siren, Dave asks, "Well, what are we going to do with this beautiful day?"

NOTES AND SOURCES

This project began in Harold Veeser's graduate Biography seminar, at the City College of New York in the spring of 2012. I want to thank Prof. Veeser for his guidance. I would also like to thank Oksana Mironova, Yelena Zolotrevskaya, and Will Crofoot for their encouragement as I continued with this project.

If not otherwise indicated, quotes are from interviews conducted by me, either in person, over the telephone, or via email. I would like to thank the following people for speaking or corresponding with me: Paul Bakija (aka Paul Cripple), Mike Edison, Russell Zanca, Steve Wishnia, Nicky Garatt, Abraham Rodriguez, Susan Cordon Bull, Fly Content, Spike Polite, Craig Flanigan, and Daphna Ariel. I would also like to thank the many other people who spoke to me informally or off the record, but still added to my understanding of this time and place.

Finally, I would like to thank Dave Powell for his assistance as I began this project, and the ABC no RIO zine library for their preservation of important cultural documents.

In addition to interviews, I have relied on the following texts:

Anders, Wadyslaw. *An Army In Exile: The Making of the Second Polish Corps.* Nashville: The Battery Press, 1981.

Anderson, Lincoln. "Michael Shenker, squatter, activist, is dead at age 54." *The Villager*. Oct. 7-13, 2010. Retrieved from thevillager.com/villager_389/michaelshenker.html Web.

Avakian, Bob. *A Reflection on the "Occupy" Movement: An Inspiring Beginning... and the Need to Go Further.* Revolution #250, November 13, 2011.

Avrich, Paul. *Anarchist Voices: An Oral History of Anarchism in America.* Abridged Edition. New Jersey: Princeton University Press, 1996.

Axel-Lute, Miriam. "Battle Over 13th Street." *Shelterforce*. May/June 1995

Bakija, Paul. I'm The Living Proof of Reagan's Lies. http://paulcripple.blogspot.com/ New York: 2012. Web.

Bakija, Paul. Interviewed by Cubesville. *Cubesville*. http://www.mixcloud.com/cubesville/paul-from-reagan-youth-interviewed-in-tompkins-square-park/ Web.

Black Eye. #8. New York: 1988.

Blush, Steven. *American Hardcore: A Tribal History.* Los Angeles: Feral House, 2001.

Counter Culture Zine. https://www.facebook.com/people/JaeMonroe/714193041#!/photo.php?fbid=1049562096123&set=a.1049544815691.6 553.1737864076&type=3&theater Web.

Damage, Donna. Interviewed by Mad At The World. *Mad At The World.* http://danscheme.blogspot.com/2007/03/interview-donna-damage-of-no- thanks.html Mad At The World, 2007. Web.

Dekel, Mikhal. "Tehran Kids." 2012: *The Global and the Intimate: Feminism in Our Time.* Eds., Geraldine Pratt and Victoria Rosner. New York, Columbia University Press.

Duncombe, Stepehen, and Tremblay, Maxwell, eds. *White Riot: Punk Rock and the Politics of Race.* London: Verso, 2011.

Edison, Mike. *I Have Fun Everywhere I Go.* New York: Faber and Faber, 2008.

False Prophets. Interview. *Maximum Rock N Roll.* Issue #46. March, 1987.

Hoffman, Abbie. *Revolution For the Hell of It.* New York: Dial Press, 1968.

Jennen, Hal. Life After Death. New York: WNYU-FM, 1982.

Jackson, Kenneth T., ed. *The Encyclopedia of New York City.* New Haven: Yale University Press, 1995.

Joseph, John. *The Evolution of a Cro-Magnon.* New York: PUNKHOuse, 2007.

Kasindorg, Jean Russell. "The Bad Seed." *New York Magazine.* 9 August 1993: 38-45.

Kraut. Interview with Suburban Punk. *Suburban Punk.* Issue #5, Spring, 1983. Retrieved from https://files.nyu.edu/cch223/public/usa/info/kraut_SVinter.html

Law, Vikki. *enter the nineties: punks, poets, politics.* 2005

Lord Ezec. Interviewed by Mass Appeal. *Mass Appeal*. July 9, 2012. Retrieved from massappeal.com/interview-with-hardcore-superstar-lord-ezec-of-the-dms-crew/2/ Web.

New York Thrash. ROIR. 1998. CD

McFadden, Robert J. "Park Curfew Protest Erupts Into a Battle And 38 Are Injured." *The New York Times.* 8 Aug. 1988.

O'Donoghue, Brian. "D-Day Hits Lower E. Side Drug Trade; Heat Stays On." *The Villager* 2 Feb. 1984.

O'Hara, Craig. *The Philosophy of Punk: More Than Noise!* San Francisco: AK Press, 1999.

Patterson, Clayton, ed. *Resistance: A Radical and Political History of the Lower East Side.* New York: Seven Stories Press, 2007.

Reagan Youth. A Collection of Pop Classics. New Red Archives, 1994. CD.

Reagan Youth. Live & Rare. New Red Archives,1998. CD.

Reagan Youth. Interviewed by Bob Z. *Bad Newz* #7, 1987.

Reagan Youth. Interviewed by Lyle Hyson, Paul Praver, Carly Sommerstein. *Maximum Rocknroll* #04 (Feb. 1983).

Reagan Youth. Reagan Youth Myspace Page. http://www.myspace.com/reaganyouth

Rettman, Tony. "Gleefully Violent Hardcore Nostalgia Reigns at the A7 Reunion." *The Village Voice*: 3 Dec. 2008. http://www.villagevoice.com/2008-12-03/music/gleefully-violent-hardcore-nostalgia-reigns-at-the-a7-reunion/full/

Rodriguez, Abraham. Interview. *Artcore* #6, 1988.

Rodriguez, Abraham. *untitled column. Oxblood.* Berlin: Oxblood, 2011.

Sabater, Dan. *A Brief History of NYC Anarchist Bookstores. The New York Independent Media* Center, 2006.

Shapiro, Gary. "New York's Oldest Anarchist Book Club Tries To Get Organized." *The Arty Semite (blog), The Jewish Daily Forward*. 30 June 2011. Web.

Social Security Administration. Social Security Death Index, Master File. Social Security Administration.

Soundex Index to Petitions for Naturalization filed in Federal, State, and Local Courts located in New York City, 1792-1989. New York, NY, USA: National Archives and Records Administration, Northeast Region.

Trunk, Isaiah. *Lodz Ghetto.* Bloomington and Indianapolis: Indiana University Press, 2006.

United States Holocaust Memorial Museum. *Holocaust Encyclopedia*. Washington DC: USHMM, 2011. Web.

Vaucher, Gee. Interview. *The Quietus*, December 2, 2012. Retrieved from http://thequietus.com/articles/10865-gee-vaucher-crass-art-interview